Water Pennies

and Other Poems

Water Pennies

and Other Poems

BY

N. M. Bodecker

ILLUSTRATED BY ERIK BLEGVAD

A MARGARET K. McELDERRY BOOK

New York

MAXWELL MACMILLAN CANADA

TORONTO

MAXWELL MACMILLAN

INTERNATIONAL

NEW YORK   OXFORD   SINGAPORE   SYDNEY

The sketches on page 53 were made by N. M. Bodecker
when he planned to illustrate
Water Pennies *himself. His death in 1988 prevented him*
from carrying out this plan.

First edition 1991
Text copyright © 1989 by Tumbledown Editions
Illustrations copyright © 1991 by Erik Blegvad

Margaret K. McElderry Books
Macmillan Publishing Company
866 Third Avenue
New York, NY 10022

Maxwell Macmillan Canada, Inc.
1200 Eglinton Avenue East
Suite 200
Don Mills, Ontario M3C 3N1

Printed in the United States of America
10 9 8 7 6 5 4 3 2 1

Library of Congress Cataloging-in-Publication Data
Bodecker, N. M.
Water pennies and other poems / by N. M. Bodecker.—1st ed.
     p.   cm.
Summary: A collection of poems featuring such small creatures
as the pollywog, snail, moth, and earthworm.
ISBN 0-689-50517-5
1. Insects—Juvenile poetry.   2. Animals—Juvenile poetry.
3. Children's poetry, American. [1. Animals—
Poetry.   2. American poetry.] I. Blegvad, Erik, Ill.   II. Title.
PS3552.O33W38   1991   811'.54—dc20   90-6477

To Pernille Bjerrehuus

Contents

Water
Pennies

and Other Poems

WATER PENNIES*

I found
a rusty
can,
or tin,
to keep
my water
pennies
in.

I kept
them there
all morning,
which
made me
feel just
a *little*
rich.

How could
that big
dog know
he drank
my water
penny
piggy
bank?

* A water penny is a tiny freshwater creature that
spends its life squirming—*NMB*.

SUMMER SKATERS*

Some skaters skate
on skates on ice
when winter's stars
and frost moons rise.

Some wait until
the ice is gone
—then happily
they skate on none.

From early dawn
they skim the pond
when shadbush blooms
in woods beyond.

"Look, look," they cry,
"how well we do:
no ice, no skates
—and barefoot too. . . .

When ice returns
they run away
—perhaps to skate
another day.

* A skater is a mosquitolike surface skimmer that
  sticks around until first frost—*NMB*.

SEEING A DRAGONFLY OVER THE POND ON A SUNNY JUNE MORNING

So dragonfly
is on
the wing,
the shiny
helicopter
thing.

Brand-new
today,
and bold
as brass,
but clear
and brittle
as fine
glass.

Untiring
it hovers
there,
a shimmering
of light
and air.

Drops to
the water;
leaves
a ring;
rises
and passes
glittering.

A miracle
of joy
—and yet,
it is
a dragon.
Don't
forget.

An inchworm
walked
a bit
of string,
and as
she walked
I heard
her sing

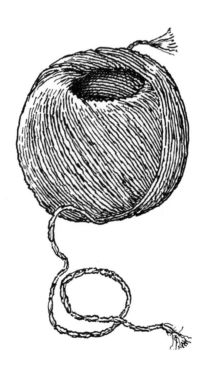

a song
of measured
joy
and sense
(each sings
her
own
experience).

And this
was her
contented
song:
"Today
was nineteen
inches
long."

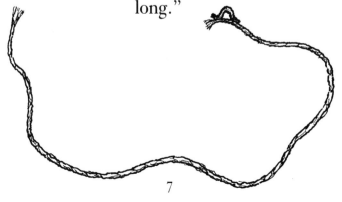

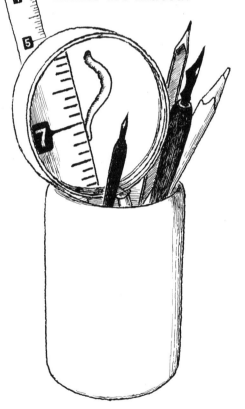

"I wonder why
the inchworm
uses inches:
Oldfangled
nonsense
inches are indeed.

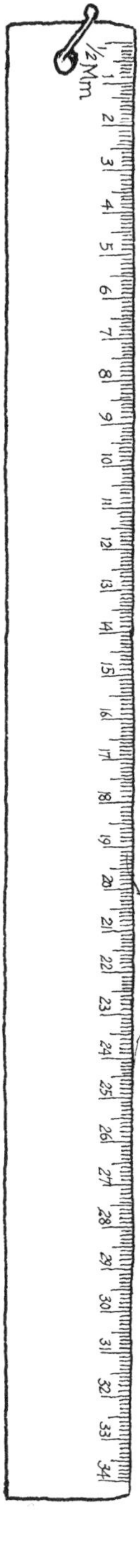

"I keep in step—
one must; and
things move swiftly
—once one goes
metric,"
said the centipede.

DADDY LONGLEGS

Oh, Daddy Longlegs,
speak to me,
you walk about
so awkwardly.

Is it your shoes
that are too tight?
Or are you dizzy
from the height?

It must be hard
to live that way,
I mean to walk
on stilts all day.

You find that
tiring? Me too;
but don't one get
a splendid view?

Always up there,
on top of things;
near birds, and clouds,
and kites on strings. . . .

Oh, tell me, Dad,
what you can see;
please, Daddy Longlegs,
speak to me.

Grasshopper high-jumps,
grasshopper low,
hop-skip-a-jump jumper
go—go—go. . . .

Up to the tippy-top
way down . . . "Joe,
where did your hop-skip-a-jump
jumper go?"

Pollywoggle-wiggle,
polly woggle-woe,
pollywoggle
          oops!
               splash!
—where did Polly go?

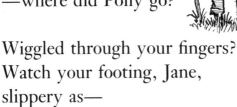

Wiggled through your fingers?
Watch your footing, Jane,
slippery as—
          oops!
               splash!
—there she goes again. . . .

BUTTERFLY

I catch
a glimpse,
and wonder
why
that thing
is called
a butterfly.

To me,
at least,
that passing
flutter
resembles
neither fly
nor butter.

But
presently,
the thought
occurs:
the name,
of course,
could have
been worse.

14

Lardwing
(perhaps)
or
goosefatfly,
or
margarinemosquito—
I
think I
shall stick
with flying
butter
—unless,
of course,
the days
get hotter.

For who
would want
his summer
sky
a-drip
with melted
butterfly?

OARSMAN*

The oarsman dips
his oars. How well
he moves his slender
racing shell,

as if in some swift
race of sorts
(why shouldn't insects
have their sports?—

for gnats, and newts,
and nymphs to see
—to win or lose
as it may be).

But this one rows
a lonely race,
and when he finds
a sunny place,

glides silently
into a pause—
an oarsman resting
on his oars,

well pleased with such
a summer's day
(he won't win any
gold *that* way).

But is it not enough
he won
this golden moment
in the sun?

* An oarsman is a bug that moves across the
surfaces of ponds and streams using its fringed,
oarlike hind legs—*NMB*.

DRIFTING SUMMER

There is a small, gray spider
who travels on a thread
all summer, over seas of green fields
    drifting.
If you should ask him where
he goes, he'd answer: "There.
Wherever summer's lazy winds are
    shifting."

But now the fields are empty,
the mist is in the corn,
and rain plays on the roof, the
    autumn's drummer.
On sunny days his thread
still passes overhead
—I wonder where it ends, his
    drifting summer?

THE SUMMER MORNING SNAIL

The summer morning snail
she leaves a shiny trail.
At sunrise in the chill, wet grass I
    find her;
so I shall always know
wherever she may go,
she leaves that guiding silver thread
    behind her.

For long before it's day
she's up and on her way,
the moon still in the pale dawn sky
    above her;
if I could be a snail,
I'd hurry on her trail,
to tell her just how very much I
    love her.

OF EYES AND EARS

The snail has eyes
on long, thin stems:
were I a snail, my dear,
I'd use my eye
to scratch myself
behind my itchy ear.

But if you were
a snail, my sweet,
in someone's cabbage patch,
you couldn't scratch
your ear because
you'd have no ear to scratch.

Well, some have eyes
that grow on stems,
and some have ears that itch;
I guess, perhaps,
that having both
would be a bit too rich.

LACEWING

The lacewing
drifts
along, you guess,
in sheerest,
lacy
laziness.

But don't be
fooled;
she hunts with zest,
as predatory
as
the rest.

SLUGS

Slugs are
peaceful, quiet
little fellows,
who have their
little sluggish tiffs
no doubt,
but hardly ever
bother
one another,
and never,
ever
stop
to slug it out.

There's no commotion
among slugs
to speak of;
they do not
jump
when taken
by surprise—
just carry on,
as steady
as the hours.

You think
that being
slow
did make them
wise?

MOTHS

They come
as evening's
shadows
fall,
small flights
of moths,
charwomen
all,

to dust
the windows,
tidy things,
and shake
their little
dust cloth
wings.

Come over
here
and you
will see:
they sweep
the windows
busily,

till dusk
is come,
all dusty
gray.
The moths
make night
—or so
we say.

A SONG TO SING TO A LADYBIRD LANDING ON YOUR SLEEVE ON A CLOUDY DAY

Ladybird,
ladybird,
Mary's speckled hen,
fly up to our Lord
and ask
for sunny skies again.

For sunshine
in the morning,
to warm the honeybee;
and white rain
in the evening
to sing its song to me.

TANK

It looked a little
like a tiny
armadillo;
the children found it
and cried:
"Look! A tank. . . ."
I thought
perhaps
it was an armored
beetle
taking money
to the bank.

THE RHINOCEROS BEETLE
AND THE LOOKING GLASS

A rhinoceros beetle
looked at itself
in a glass
it had found
and said:
"Ugh!
I thought
I was
quite—
THE RHINOCEROS!

but—
it appears
I am only
a bug. . . ."

"Glowworm," said the firefly,
"you are so very slow;
I light a hundred fires
while *you* just sit and glow.

"You should be up and doing;
I flit from tree to tree
—folks must be quick and nimble
if they'll catch up with *me*."

"Yes," said the glowworm slowly,
"indeed, one wonders why
the Lord made one a glowworm,
and one a firefly.

"*You* flicker (it's your nature,
and such a lovely sight),
my glow is low and steady
—that, too, is quite all right.

"All things must be in balance
for life to function well;
some must be entertaining
—some just dependable."

Mayfly and June bug
each have their season;
they come and they go
for no very clear reason.

Perhaps they are simply
good neighbors, the two,
meeting as briefly
as Mays and Junes do.

Summer guests, really,
polite as you please;
one likes the roses,
and one the sweet peas.

One opens "June House"
as one shuts "Camp May";
one says, "Good-bye, now"
as one says, "Good day."

Touch feelers in passing:
"How lovely, my dear.
Must run, though, but see you
same time/place next year."

Oh, Mayflies and June bugs,
they come and they go . . .
to meet once a year
makes good neighbors, you know.

BEHAVE

Bees are busy,
sincere, and grave;
from dawn till sunset
they strive and slave.
They brook no nonsense,
so do behave!
When passing their hive,
before or behind,
be good,
be quiet,
be always kind.
For yours may well
be the skin
you save!
So, dear,
near the *bee*hive
be*have*.
BEHAVE!

For if there be one thing
that bees do crave,
it's privacy
in their hive or cave.
So when you are passing
behind or before
the bee-queen's castle
or bee-drone's door,
be wary,
be watchful,
beware, dear, or
you may get a lick
or a wee bee-stare!
Oh, dear,
near the *bee*hive
be*have*.
BEHAVE!

SHOOING A FLY OFF HIS CHAIR
BEFORE SITTING DOWN TO WORK

Excuse me, fly,
I meant not to disturb you;
but this, as it so happens,
is *my* chair.
Sit somewhere else;
the wall, the floor, the ceiling;
sit anywhere you please
—except not *there*. . . .

Not on my *nose*,
you nut; not on my *finger;*
not on my bald spot, numbskull;
leave me be!
I didn't sit on *you*
when *you* were sitting.
So why on earth should *you*
now sit on *me*?

WHATSHAMACALLIT

Whatshamacallit
came over the doorstep. . . .
Whatshamacallit
went under a straw. . . .
Whatshamacallit
had shiny, black feelers. . . .
I *never* saw such an odd bodkin
   before.

Whatshamacallit
climbed up on my sneaker. . . .
Whatshamacallit
said: "How-do-you-do?"
Whatshamacallit
said: "Lor', if you please, sir,
I *never* saw such a spectacular
   view. . . ."

Whatshamacallit
went down to the village. . . .
Whatshamacallit
was sort of a friend. . . .
Whatshamacallit
got talking to someone
and never came back to me.
Ever. The End.

THE TOAD

There hopped
across
the rainy
road
a small,
we thought,
quite ugly
toad.

Then thought
again:
"Could we
be dumb?
This toad
is handsome
to its
mom.

"And she
to him,
no doubt,
no less
(toads have
their kind
of loveliness).

"It's all
in the
beholder's
eye;
and so,
most handsome
toad,
'Good-bye.' "

OF TOADS AND TOADSTOOLS

Toadstools may
be lots of fun
for tired toads
to sit down on;
and yet I never
came upon,
in all my life
(said Uncle John)
a single toad
who sat on one.

Nor one on which
(said Auntie Pat)
a tired toad
had ever sat;
for which the reason
may be that:
stools are
too high,
or toads
too fat.

THE EARTHWORM

Earthworm,
my friend
of silent toil,
you ate
rank dirt
to make
sweet soil.

'Twas good
for me:
my gardens
grew
—but how
could it
be good
for you?

44

PILL BEETLE

The little
beetle
they call
pill
needs
no vet
when he
is ill.

Whatever shape
you find
him in,
he is
his own
best medicine.

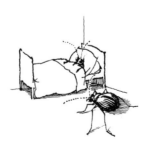

SILVERFISH

The silverfish
is not a fish,
and you should be
suspicious
if someone says
that silverfish
with parsley is
delicious.

MIDSUMMER NIGHT ITCH

Mosquito is out,
it's the end of the day;
she's humming and hunting
her evening away.

Who knows why such hunger
arrives on such wings
at sundown? I guess
it's the nature of things.

OF GNATS AND BATS

"A gnat
should not,
you know,"
said Nat,
"get up
to breakfast
with a bat.

"It matters
not
the least,
at that,
if Mister
Gnat
be fit,
or fat,

"or lean,
or mean,
or thin,
or flat;
for bat
eats gnat,
and that
is that."

THE LOUSE, THE NIGHT,
AND THE STAR

The lowly
louse
has his
small house,
and in-laws,
cousins,
kids,
and spouse.

But sometimes
sits,
when all
sleep tight,
a louse
alone
with skies
at night.

And asks
again:
"Bright
evening
star,
why *am*
I so
unpopular?"

N. M. BODECKER was born in Denmark and studied at the School of Architecture and the School of Applied Arts in Copenhagen. His first collection of poetry was published in Denmark when he was nineteen. Some years later, he moved to the United States, where he made his living as an illustrator, working on his poetry "after hours." With the publication in 1974 of *Let's Marry Said the Cherry* (a McElderry Book), he returned to both writing and illustrating his own works. The recipient of numerous awards, Mr. Bodecker wrote fifteen books and illustrated over forty. He died in 1988.

ERIK BLEGVAD was born in Denmark and studied there at the School of Applied Arts in Copenhagen. After serving in the Royal Danish Air Force during World World II, he moved to Paris, where he worked for various publications. Mr. Blegvad has illustrated over seventy children's books and drawn for numerous magazines. He and his wife, Lenore, a children's book author, now divide their time between Vermont in the United States and London, England.

European Earwig

N

The copepod
is rather od.